Totally Dinosaurs

BY DENNIS SCHATZ

ILLUSTRATIONS BY
BOB GREISEN

To Jim and Ron, who always encouraged my activities in science.

Silver Dolphin Books
An imprint of the Baker & Taylor Publishing Group
10350 Barnes Canyon Road, San Diego, CA 92121
www.silverdolphinbooks.com

ISBN-13: 978-1-60710-785-9
ISBN-10: 1-60710-785-6

Totally Dinosaurs is produced by becker&mayer!, Bellevue, Washington
www.beckermayer.com

Manufactured, printed, and assembled in He Yuan City, China.

1 2 3 4 5 17 16 15 14 13

12464

Fact card writer: Robin Cruise
Fact card editor: Betsy Henry Pringle
Edited by Jennifer Doyle
Book designers: Two Pollard Design
Cover designer: Scott Westgard
Typesetting by Sheila Van Nortwick
Photo researcher: Kara Stokes
Production coordinator: Diane Ross

Photo Credits: Cards and Poster: Pteranodon © Linda Bucklin/Shutterstock; Brachiosaurus © Catmando/Shutterstock; Compsognathus © Linda Bucklin/Shutterstock; Camarasaurus © Andreas Meyer/Shutterstock; Deinonychus © Michael Rosskothen/Shutterstock; Apatosaurus © Linda Bucklin/Shutterstock; Ankylosaurus © Leonello Calvetti/Shutterstock; Ankylosaurus background © Kirschner/Shutterstock; Carnotaurus © Coreyford/Dreamstime; Ceratosaurus © Kostyantyn Ivanyshen/Shutterstock; Diplodocus © Catmando/Shutterstock; Euoplocephalus © Ralf Juergen Kraft/Shutterstock; Euoplocephalus background © Michael Rosskothen/ Shutterstock; Gigantoraptor © Kostyantyn Ivanyshen/Shutterstock; Kentrosaurus © Kostyantyn Ivanyshen/Shutterstock; Monolophosaurus © Kostyantyn Ivanyshen/Shutterstock; Oviraptor © Kostyantyn Ivanyshen/Shutterstock; Oviraptor background © Kostyantyn Ivanyshen/Shutterstock; Pachycephalosaurus © Leonello Calvetti/Shutterstock; Pachycephalosaurus background © Kostyantyn Ivanyshen/Shutterstock; Parasaurolophus © Jean-Michel Girard/Shutterstock; Parasaurolophus background © Catmando/Shutterstock; Psittacosaurus © Linda Bucklin/Shutterstock; Spinosaurus © Kostyantyn Ivanyshen/ Shutterstock; Stegosaurus © TsuneoMP/Shutterstock; Suchomimus © Kostyantyn Ivanyshen/ Shutterstock; Triceratops © Ralf Juergen Kraft/Shutterstock; Triceratops background © Kostyantyn Ivanyshen/Shutterstock; Tyrannosaurus rex © TsuneoMP/Shutterstock; Tyrannosaurus rex background © Andreas Meyer/Shutterstock; Velociraptor © Michael Rosskothen/Shutterstock.

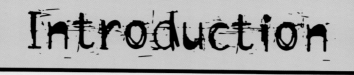

Introduction

Imagine yourself a scientist studying dinosaurs, piecing together the skeletons of giant animals that roamed the earth millions of years ago. The collection of bones in this kit lets you do just that.

Follow the easy, step-by-step instructions on the next four pages to build five different dinosaurs: Apatosaurus, Stegosaurus, Velociraptor, Triceratops, and Tyrannosaurus rex. The dinosaurs you can build using this kit will all be about the same size, so you can mix and match parts to create new kinds of dinosaurs. Here is a comparison of their real sizes.

Assembly Instructions

Put Apatosaurus, Stegosaurus, Velociraptor, Triceratops, and Tyrannosaurus rex back together again! First try building one dinosaur at a time, then build two dinosaurs at once—mix a Stegosaurus or Triceratops with a Velociraptor or Tyrannosaurus rex. Since the bones can be mixed and matched, you can also create new kinds of dinosaurs. Who knows? Scientists may one day discover the fossil of a dinosaur that looks exactly like one you dreamed up in your imagination.

Each dinosaur bone corresponds with a number, as shown on the Bone Map included in your kit. There are two illustrations of each dinosaur: a number-by-number guide to fitting the bones together, and a picture of what the skeleton should look like once it's assembled.

Apatosaurus

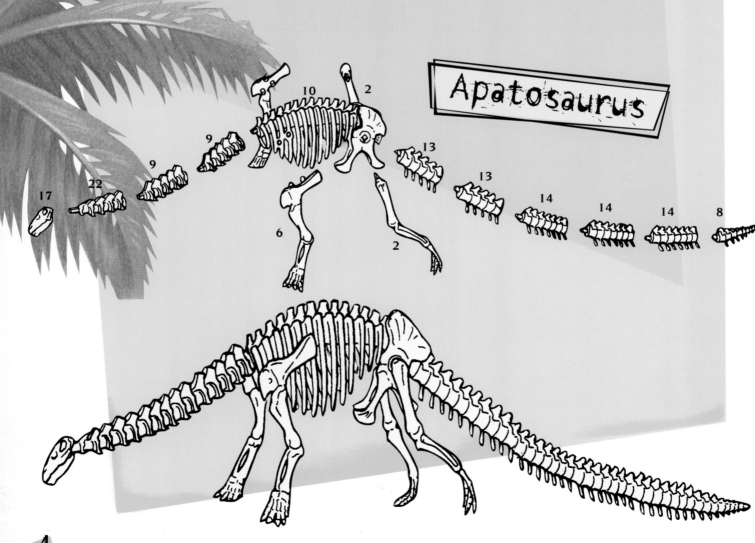

Stegosaurus

Velociraptor

5

Triceratops

Tyrannosaurus rex

When Dinosaurs Ruled the Earth

Between 225 and 65 million years ago, dinosaurs ruled the earth. Some were as large as houses, while others were no bigger than chickens. Herds of thousands of plant-eating dinosaurs roamed the land, their thundering movements heard and felt for miles. Their bleating and roaring overpowered all other sounds. Packs of meat-eating dinosaurs scanned the herds from high ground, searching for stragglers or injured animals for that night's dinner. The sky periodically darkened as flocks of giant pterosaurs (tair-uh-SAWRs)—some the size of small airplanes—passed overhead, migrating to distant feeding grounds.

No humans lived on Earth. No large mammals such as elephants or bears existed. Most mammals were small—some the distant relatives of the rat—and they came out only at night.

That all changed 65 million years ago.

Mammals vs. Dinosaurs

Mammals are born alive and feed on milk from their mothers' bodies. Most dinosaurs had babies that hatched from eggs. Their bones were like those of today's birds, which is why many scientists think birds are descendants of the dinosaurs.

9

The Last Days of the Dinosaurs

Sixty-five million years ago, Earth collided with either an asteroid or a comet that was four miles wide. Traveling at more than 100,000 miles per hour—faster than a speeding bullet—this messenger of destruction plowed into what is now the Gulf of Mexico.

The space rock blasted a hole in the earth that stretched hundreds of miles across—bigger than the state of Washington. The explosion threw rock and dirt into the air, which spread around the earth and blocked out the sun. An eerie darkness set in everywhere for months. Without sunlight, temperatures dropped dramatically. Most plants could no longer exist. Much of life on Earth died out, including all the dinosaurs.

How do we know dinosaurs existed if they have not been around for millions of years? Figuring this out is like solving a mystery. Dinosaur bones buried in the ground—called *fossils*—give us clues as to what dinosaurs were like. Not all the bones of each dinosaur are found, but scientists can use the bones they do discover to figure out how big each dinosaur was, what it ate, and how it looked. Turn the page and journey back more than 100 million years to discover what it was like in the days of the dinosaurs.

Asteroids and Comets

An asteroid is solid rock, while a comet is like a dirty snowball. Both are leftover building materials from the formation of our solar system. Billions of comets and asteroids travel around our Sun, but only rarely do they collide with Earth.

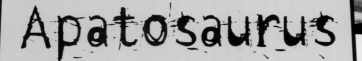

Apatosaurus

Nearly 150 million years ago, gigantic dinosaurs roamed the earth. An Apatosaurus gently moves through a grove of pine trees that stand more than one hundred feet tall—as tall as ten-story buildings. Even with heavily padded feet, she causes the ground to shake with each step. Towering above the land, she swings her head through the air in search of the trees with the most needles. Her neck is long enough to reach hard-to-get needles left by earlier feeders. She balances back on her tail and places her front legs on the side of a tree. With one smooth movement, her peg-like front teeth clamp down on a branch and strip off all the needles. Having no molars, she swallows her food whole.

After satisfying her hunger, the Apatosaurus roams off to a quiet, shaded area, where she lays down for a midday nap. As she rests, the large stones in her gizzard do what molars do in other dinosaurs—grind up the tough needles so her stomach can digest the food.

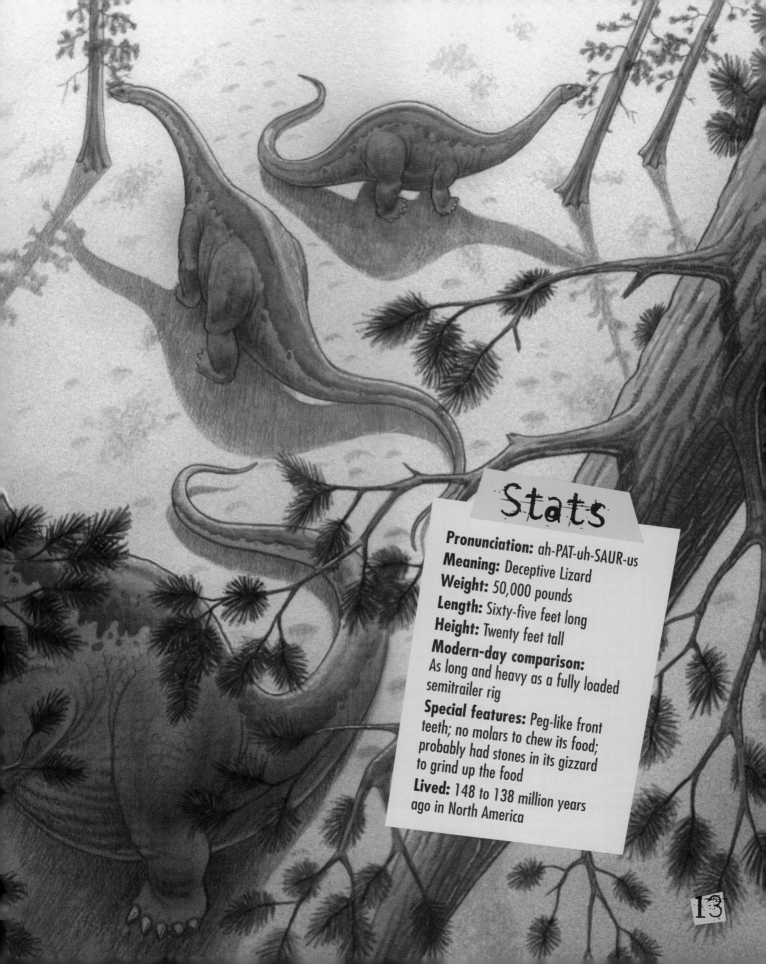

Stats

Pronunciation: ah-PAT-uh-SAUR-us

Meaning: Deceptive Lizard

Weight: 50,000 pounds

Length: Sixty-five feet long

Height: Twenty feet tall

Modern-day comparison: As long and heavy as a fully loaded semitrailer rig

Special features: Peg-like front teeth; no molars to chew its food; probably had stones in its gizzard to grind up the food

Lived: 148 to 138 million years ago in North America

13

Stegosaurus

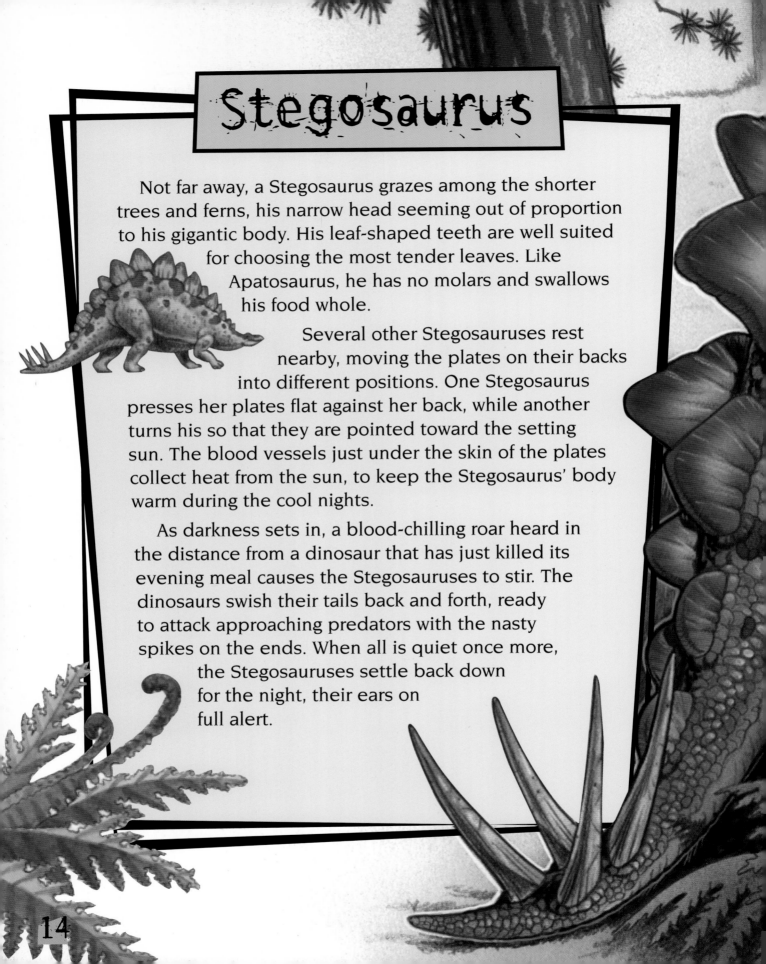

Not far away, a Stegosaurus grazes among the shorter trees and ferns, his narrow head seeming out of proportion to his gigantic body. His leaf-shaped teeth are well suited for choosing the most tender leaves. Like Apatosaurus, he has no molars and swallows his food whole.

Several other Stegosauruses rest nearby, moving the plates on their backs into different positions. One Stegosaurus presses her plates flat against her back, while another turns his so that they are pointed toward the setting sun. The blood vessels just under the skin of the plates collect heat from the sun, to keep the Stegosaurus' body warm during the cool nights.

As darkness sets in, a blood-chilling roar heard in the distance from a dinosaur that has just killed its evening meal causes the Stegosauruses to stir. The dinosaurs swish their tails back and forth, ready to attack approaching predators with the nasty spikes on the ends. When all is quiet once more, the Stegosauruses settle back down for the night, their ears on full alert.

Stats

Pronunciation: STEG-uh-SAWR-us

Meaning: Plated Lizard

Weight: 4,000 pounds

Length: More than twenty feet long

Height: More than twenty feet tall

Modern-day comparison: Plates on back acted like solar-powered water heaters. Instead of heating water, the sun's energy heated the Stegosaurus' blood

Special features: Two rows of fifteen to twenty-five large plates along its back; four spikes on the end of its tail

Lived: 152 to 142 million years ago in North America

Velociraptor

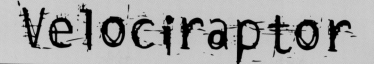

Now let's travel forward more than 50 million years, where thousands of miles away in what is now Mongolia, a group of newborn baby Velociraptors is cared for by several adults. One adult is pushing from the den broken eggshells left from the babies' recent hatching.

Outside, several young Velociraptors practice their hunting skills. They are not as big as the adults, but the long, curved claws on the inside of each hind foot are fully developed. They practice moving these long claws, swinging them out of the way when running and moving them in a wide arc while jumping into the air, like they do when cutting into the bodies of prey. The Velociraptors playfully hook their front claws onto one another—much more gently than when they use them to hold down prey while their rear claws slice it open.

Stats

Pronunciation: veh-loss-ih-RAP-tor

Meaning: Swift Plunderer

Weight: Up to 500 pounds

Length: Six feet long

Height: Three feet tall

Modern-day comparison: Bigger than a chopper motorcycle

Special features: Walked on two legs; ten-inch claws—the size of steak knives—on the inside toe of each hind foot

Lived: 78 to 70 million years ago in Mongolia

Parasaurolophus

A mother Parasaurolophus watches over twelve baby dinosaurs that are just emerging from their eggs. Months before, she laid the eggs in her nest in two straight lines. Some of the eggs, not yet hatched, are still covered with thick plant material to keep them warm.

Agitated by the bellowing coming from two dinosaurs dueling nearby, the Parasaurolophus rises up on her hind legs and extends her head high. She makes a deep, trombone-like sound out of the tube that connects the top of her head to her nose—a signal to her mate to return to the nest. Her mate comes galloping back, still chewing the plants he picked to soften them up for transfer to the mouths of the helpless baby dinosaurs. As he arrives at the nest, the babies lift their heads and open their mouths in anticipation of the food he brings whenever he returns.

Stats

Pronunciation:
par-uh-sawr-OL-uh-fuss
Meaning: Two-Ridged Lizard
Weight: 5,000 pounds
Length: Thirty feet long
Height: Eighteen feet tall
Modern-day comparison: Twice as big as a full-grown giraffe
Special feature: Tube on top of head connected to its nose created a trombone-like sound; mouth had a bony ridge to snip off plants
Lived: 80 to 65 million years ago in North America

Stats

Pronunciation: try-SAIR-uh-tops

Meaning: Three-Horned Face

Weight: 10,000 pounds

Length: Thirty feet long

Height: Thirteen feet tall

Modern-day comparison: Bigger than a large van

Special features: Head had three horns on the front and a large, bony shield—called a *frill*—on the back

Lived: 72 to 65 million years ago in North America

Triceratops

A herd of 500 Triceratops eats dinner from the low bushes near the bank of a river in what is now the state of Montana. The sound of cracking wood fills the air as the Triceratops use their sharp beaks to snap off thick branches other dinosaurs can't eat. They are still grinding up the tough plant material with their massive molars as they move toward the shallow water for a drink.

On their way to the riverbed, a group of adult and baby Triceratops gets separated from the rest of the herd. Three hungry Dromaeosauruses quietly watching from a nearby hill seize this opportunity to attack, hoping to make a meal of one of the Triceratops. A full-grown Triceratops will provide more than enough food for the entire pack of Dromaeosauruses.

Dromaeosaurus

With a series of loud yelps, the Dromaeosauruses attack one of the straggling adult Triceratops. The predators pounce from three sides at once, leaping high to make long slashes with their sharp hind claws along the back side of the Triceratops. The deep gashes begin to spurt blood. This merely angers the Triceratops. He charges the Dromaeosauruses like a rhinoceros, using the two horns over his eyes—each one longer than a baseball bat—as weapons.

One of the Dromaeosauruses goes after the Triceratops' neck, where veins carrying blood are near the surface. But the Triceratops snaps back his head, covering his neck with the bony frill on the back. The Dromaeosaurus' blow falls harmlessly, with a loud *thud*. Several of the adult Triceratops charge the Dromaeosauruses, trying to scare off the dinosaurs with their long horns. The other adults in the group circle around the babies, bellowing loudly.

This noise does not escape the attention of another dinosaur in search of an evening meal.

Stats

Pronunciation:
DROM-ee-uh-sawr-us

Meaning: Running Lizard

Weight: Up to 500 pounds

Length: Six feet long

Height: Three feet tall

Modern-day comparison:
Bigger than a chopper motorcycle

Special feature: Looked just like Velociraptor, but with a wider head

Lived: 78 to 70 million years ago in North America

Tyrannosaurus Rex

Tyrannosaurus rex, the largest meat-eater ever to walk the earth, is king of all the dinosaurs that live by the river. He is walking along the riverbank when he hears the yelps and roars of the Dromaeosaurus and Triceratops. His giant head slowly swivels in that direction. His bulging eyes rotate forward, giving him the sharp vision needed to scan the horizon for food. His sensitive nose, which can detect the scent of blood as far away as twenty miles, smells the blood seeping from the wounded Triceratops. He makes his way toward the fighting dinosaurs.

As the Tyrannosaurus rex stomps forward, his knees higher than your head, his massive feet sink several inches into the muddy bank with each step, producing a loud sucking sound. The three mighty claws on each of his feet are better suited for pinning down other animals than for walking in the mud.

Stats

Pronunciation: tye-RAN-uh-sawr-us rex

Meaning: Tyrant Lizard King

Weight: 8,000 pounds

Length: More than forty feet long

Height: Eighteen feet tall

Modern-day comparison: Weight and size of a small school bus

Special features: Large, sensitive nose; up to fifty seven-inch-long, curved teeth; walked on two legs; each foot had three claws, like a modern-day bird; small front legs, each with two claws

Lived: 70 to 65 million years ago in North America

T-Rex's Teeth

Tyrannosaurus rex had the perfect teeth for eating meat. Each of its fifty teeth had a sharp point and was curved toward the back of its mouth. Any prey trying to escape from Tyrannosaurus rex's grip merely pushed the teeth deeper into its skin. The back of Tyrannosaurus rex's teeth were jagged like a steak knife, to help cut through the thick flesh of its prey. When teeth were lost during a battle, new teeth grew in to replace the old ones.

Tyrannosaurus Rex
Finds Dinner

The Tyrannosaurus rex approaches the battling Triceratops and Dromaeosauruses and waits patiently for the outcome. A scavenger that lives off of dead and dying animals, he knows if the Dromaeosauruses succeed in killing the Triceratops, he will be able to feast on the tidbits of meat the Dromaeosauruses leave behind.

The Tyrannosaurus rex's patience pays off. The Triceratops succeed in driving off the Dromaeosauruses, and the stragglers set off to rejoin their herd. Soon the injured Triceratops falls behind. The Tyrannosaurus rex lumbers up on his massive hind legs to finish off the still-bleeding dinosaur. Although heavier than the Tyrannosaurus rex, the Triceratops is limping badly and can't twist his body quickly enough to charge. The Tyrannosaurus rex sinks his sharp, curved teeth into the Triceratops' neck. Exhausted, the Triceratops collapses, and the Tyrannosaurus rex is able to rip off a large chunk of meat. Having no molars to chew his food, the king of the dinosaurs swallows his first bite of dinner whole.

Ancient Records

Fossils of dinosaur footprints exist as well. The footprints of dinosaurs were usually washed away, but on rare occasions they were preserved when they quickly filled with sand or dirt before the next rain came. Over millions of years, more rock and dirt would cover the footprints. The weight of the overlying materials pressed the dried mud into stone— records of the dinosaurs waiting to be discovered millions of years later.

How Dinosaurs Became Fossils

As the Tyrannosaurus rex is about to take a second bite of the Triceratops, a flash flood produced by a thunderstorm earlier in the day rounds a bend in the river. All of a sudden the two dinosaurs are tumbling together underwater. Unable to fight their way to the surface of the fierce, rapidly flowing water, both drown. As the flood subsides, their bodies end up half buried among the mud, rocks, and bushes left behind.

Scavenger animals eat the meat from the dinosaurs' bodies, scattering their bones. The remaining flesh and soft parts of the dinosaurs rot away, leaving only the bones. Over millions of years, more floods bury the bones deeper in mud. Pressure from overlying materials such as rocks and dirt slowly turns the mud to rock. Minerals in the water that seeps into the rock fill small air spaces in the bone, turning the bones into fossils. Most of the time fossils remain hidden deep underground, but this time was different.

Discovering the Fossils

A modern-day construction crew digging into the hillside to build a new road accidentally discovers the Tyrannosaurus rex and Triceratops fossils. If you were a paleontologist, this site could be your summer workplace.

Bulldozers, jackhammers, and charges of dynamite are used to break away rock and expose the bones of the Triceratops. It's a hundred degrees in the shade, but there is no shade. The equipment kicks up clouds of dirt that mix with the sweat streaming down your face, making you look and feel grimy.

To free the bones from the ground without damaging them, your work requires a delicate touch with hand-held tools: pickaxes, shovels, hammers, and chisels. Fossils can easily break or crack when they are uncovered, so you quickly but carefully wrap them in burlap cloth soaked in plaster of Paris. This will protect the fossils like a cast does a broken bone, allowing you to load them onto a flatbed truck and transport them to your laboratory.

Studying the Dinosaurs

Scientists who study dinosaur fossils are called paleontologists (pay-lee-ahn-TAHL-uh-jists). They usually spend their summers digging up fossils, and the rest of the year in the laboratory studying their finds.

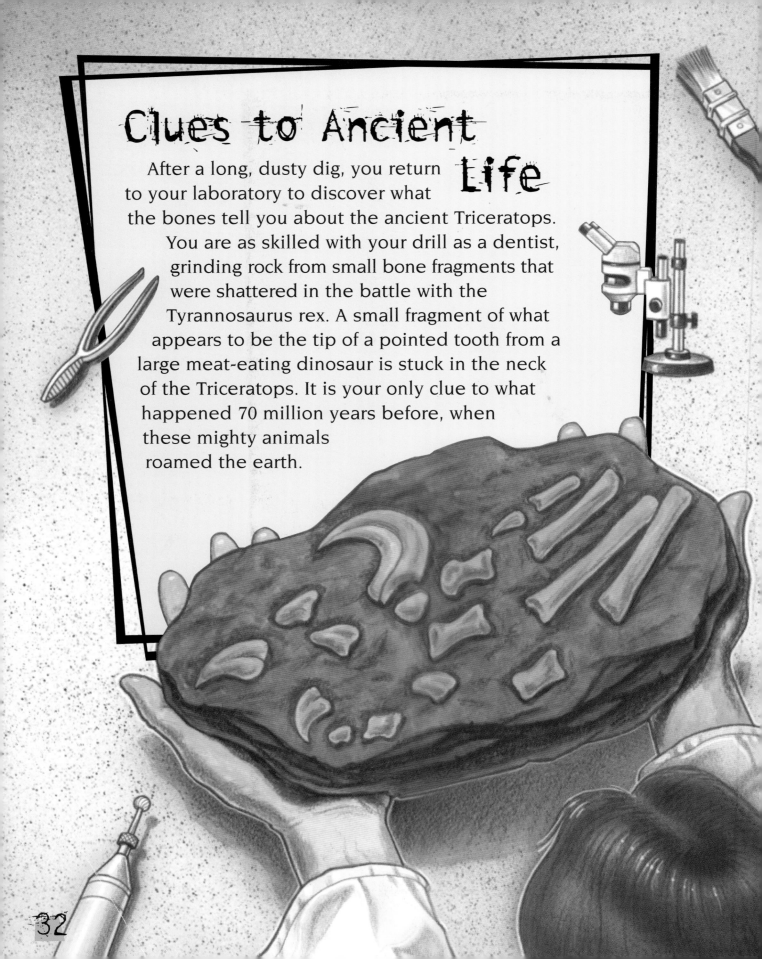

Clues to Ancient Life

After a long, dusty dig, you return to your laboratory to discover what the bones tell you about the ancient Triceratops. You are as skilled with your drill as a dentist, grinding rock from small bone fragments that were shattered in the battle with the Tyrannosaurus rex. A small fragment of what appears to be the tip of a pointed tooth from a large meat-eating dinosaur is stuck in the neck of the Triceratops. It is your only clue to what happened 70 million years before, when these mighty animals roamed the earth.